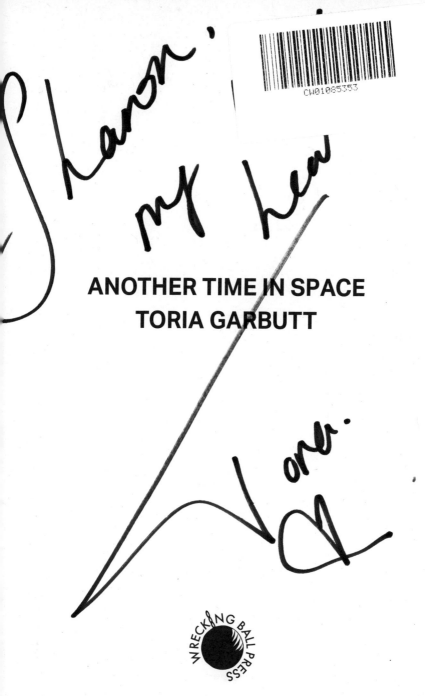

ANOTHER TIME IN SPACE
TORIA GARBUTT

WRECKING BALL PRESS

For my sister, Leanne Garbutt.
I'll see you there.

Another Time In Space
Toria Garbutt

ISBN 978-1-903110-96-6

First published in this edition 2022 by Wrecking Ball Press.

Cover design by humandesign.co.uk

Supported using public funding by
LOTTERY FUNDED | ARTS COUNCIL ENGLAND

CONTENT

LIGHTEN UP

Have a greasy fling with McDonald's hash browns
Have 4 fuck it
Dip them in ketchup on your own in the car park
Every time you see a dog, stroke it
Notice dogs appear as if by magic
Notice how you attract all dogs
Let dogs let dogs let dogs
Be the best bit of your day
Stroke a dog and you won't regret it
Get a red chin from kissing or eating apples
Av a shag in the shower
You don't have to wash the sheets after
Stand under a bridge and listen to pigeons
Remember your nanna
Remember her warming her arse on the gas fire
Remember her telling you to cure your bellyache wi a sprout sarnie
Remember her bad spelling and that text that should have read
    "I am knackered with your grandad" but instead read "I am
    naked with your grandad"
Remember her Penpal who was on death row for murder
Remember how she woke you up on a morning frantically
    knocking on your bedroom door and saying "your toast's
    getting cold"
Remember how her toast looked like it was buttered with an
    hedge strimmer
Remember how she loved it when you started smoking when
    you were 14 because it gave you a thing in common and she
    brought you 200 Marlboros back from France and your mam
    hated it but dint say owt

Remember how she made the best fucking chips in West
    Yorkshire
Remember how she got pissed off when you didn't go round for
    a couple of weeks but she'd buy you stuff anyway and then
    chuck it at you
Dance behind your door before you leave the house. Do that
    Egyptian arm thing or something stupid and have a joke
    with yourself you mad bastard
Get the bags of shopping from your boot and talk to yourself
    like this "ere y'are love, I'll get those for you"
Be your new best mate
Be your lover
Talk to yourself like an angel good as gold, proper
Lighten up cocker
Take off a load
Stop saying sorry
Start saying no

20 WEELAND ROAD

Last night,
Memories nudged their way through
I was on a walk with you
During those 18 months
You were well

You carried Laughter
Round Knottla
On your shoulders
A Statue of Liberty
Snapshot

We walked round the back of our childhood home
Number 20 Weeland Road
We were shocked how small the garden looked
We still felt it belonged to us

Our dad's redundancy money
From the Coal Board
Had paid to do it up
And we'd left in a rush

A messy ending
Too much
For both of us

This place
Always in our dreams
A need to revisit
To amend that last scene

The owner came out
And you said
Eyes wide like an expectant child
As though we might be invited in
"We useda live here when we wa little"

Outsiders once stood there
At the wall
Behind the dog pen
That our dad built

Where we both now stood

Two little girls
30 years on
Trying to take back
What still belonged to us

BATHROOM

You used to snip the silver ball
Off hair bobbles
And put them in the toothbrush cup
With water
And pretend they were fish
I useda blast the tap
Into a packet of Smiths Crisps
Once I shaved my face with our dad's razor
And cut my bottom lip

It was the 80s
In our bathroom
It was just what we did

THESE KIDS

Lad stands in line to get his book signed for a lass
Feels embarrassed
Pushes and shoves
This lad
Shoves him back
Nicks his book and launches it
Now it's on the floor
He sits back down
Kicks his chair
Says it dunt matter anymore
I go over to talk
He says he dunt care what I say
It's just another shit moment in another shit day

Lass turns her paper into planes
Over n over
Again n again
I say
That's a beautiful metaphor
For escaping pain
She says
What the fuck you on about?
And folds it up again
Holds up her poem and rips it in half
Last night she saw her brother get stabbed in the park
So I can take my fucking metaphor
And shove it up my arse

And some of them can't take the praise. I tell them WELL DONE
    "you're good at making rhymes up, ey?"
and they fold their arms and shake their heads
Wish I'd told them off instead
They tell me they come from
Shut the fuck up
And don't come back
Sausage butties
And a terrorist attack
Another says he works these streets, with his brother, selling crack
One sits and doesn't talk
One takes the piss
One asks me what car I drive
Says are you rich, miss?
These kids in the system
These kids at risk
These kids who need a cuddle
These kids these kids these kids

PUP

Remember that time
We found that dog
It followed us around
Morrison's carpark
In Ponte
We walked it home
Three miles to Knottla
And we rang the number on its collar
And the owners came to pick it up
They said
They'd been to our house
Five years before

It was our Jud and Lucy's pup

KIRKGATE

You attached me
like an umbilical cord
foetal and unformed
to your Mother city
Dripfed me on dole
Jack Fultons' frozen omlettes
Nirvana and Hole
housed me hungry and kicking
'til I was whole
then pushed me out
fully formed and screaming
ungraceful and impatient
straight onto stages
down basements
In Players
in all of their faces

We lived
this side of the subway
the dirty outskirts
a three-storey terrace
with no central heating
or curtains
a carpet that looked
ripped up from a pub
too small for the floor
lost like a hanky
sinking in mud
Plenty of room

for amps and guitars
a mattress
some candles
an artex sky of
glow in the dark stars
A pink glass ashtray
from Poundland
a centre piece
of glamour and cheap
This home on Berner's Street
for fifty quid a week

Kirkgate
Where I sobbed and sobbed on your Social Security steps
when they stopped my dole
prayed to the universe
please don't make me go home
Where we got trains to Leeds
Stood in rain and smoked
on open platforms
Cocky and soaked under
leopard print coats
swigged voddy and choked
on Marlboro Lights
stumbled
in heels
in lipstick
in limbo
in fake fake furs

in crazy crazy love
that even now
still hurts

PISS

Scunny Pete told me
Once
Someone came flying at him
With his fist
So he took out his dick
And started to piss
He thought
"surely he won't beat me up like this"

But he did

THE CRESCENT

I stood in our
Different kitchen
With zipped up
Padded
Penguin arms
Fat as an empty biscuit box
While
Mam
Hugged me

How I ached to hug her back
But could not
Such was the strength
Of his loyalty knot
How love tugged
To come out
And surround us

A week later
I met her at the Crescent
We'd never been before
Strange how separation
Creates new uncharted law
Our Greg took me in his car
I wore a flowery frock
And a straw hat
Aware even at that age
Of the cinematic
Effect of that

We sat and didn't speak
All the things
I'd hoped she'd say to me

The air con broke
During Gone With The Wind
I stripped to vest and knickers
Three hours in

A strange thing to do
In the Crescent
A strange
Strange thing

WHEN YOU DO ALL OF THOSE THINGS

Sweet sons
Turn the taps
Load the washer
Run a bath
Let me hear
The vroom
Of the vacuum
In your room
The click of the kettle

Son, do me a favour
Fill the hot water bottle
Clean the car
Empty the bin
Be a good lad n
Bring the shopping in

My lads
I am proud of you for so many things
But nothing makes me prouder
Than when you
Do all of those things

PIERROT

There must have been days in between
When your black eyes bore inwards
And you remembered
Your distant ghost self
Days when you dressed and left the flat
Resolute that you would one day soon
Come back
And in the in between
You walked into town
Eyes lined like a clown
And found
A Pierrot trinket
In a charity shop
A souvenir

From 30 years ago
From 10 miles away
From another time in space

DIFFERENT KITCHENS

cat flaps and flat caps and fash mags and handbags and
    crosswords and cross words and chip pans and nannans
    and Berkleys n doylums n cow bags n cushes n lush brown
    rugs and Kellogs cornflakes mugs n Kit Kats n tiebacks n
    big rough barking ginger dogs n dribbling spit pictures and
    licking my fingers and
My world is no bigger than the garden gate
And my world is no bigger than
the edge of our estate
And innit mad?
Innit mad what thoughts you forced in my infant head
Innit mad dreaming of freedom and waking up dead
Bleach in bins in Broomhill kitchens
dirty little bleeders and spotless kids
Willow pattern plates and Littlewood tins
that Japanese phonebook wi everyone's number in
87370 87370
sitting on t' sideboard and microwaving cheese
watching dad crying and begging please
mam coming for her stuff escorted by police
then six months later coming back for me
Curries and omelettes and feeling scared
being banged against t' worktop by t'scrag of my hair
my hamster dead
my hamster dead
drumkits and bike bits and cheap fizz and tit bits and carpet
    and cat bowls and dole holes and high heels and no meals
    not wanting to feel not wanting to feel and lines up up up
    too many times and lies and lies and hold up stockings on

baby thighs not daring to cry not daring to cry
not daring to cry

LAST DAY ON EARTH

Don't tell me
It's my last day on earth
I will only spoil it
By over planning
I know I'll get it wrong
And cry
Because it's not how I imagined
Because my idea of perfect was not right
Please for one last day and one last night
Just let us be us
Let me run big blue baths
Light incense
Fall asleep
Let me make
Hot chocolate
And kiss your silly cheeks
Let me tut at
Your daft blast of song
Let me get it wrong
And be sorry
Let me make amends
Let's laugh and laugh and keep it going for fucking ages 'til it's
    painful and I might wee
Let me have not an inkling of knowing
Only feelings of hope
Only feelings of love
Please please for one last day
and one last night
Just let us
be us

OUCH

Some people don't know what to say
So they say
I don't know what to say
And I prefer it that way
Some people ask questions
Like "was it cancer?"
When I say it was not
Some react odd
Draw in their breath
And say "ouch"
As though my car repair
Was costly
Ouch
As if I've been stung
Ouch
As if the thing can be
Fixed with a plaster
And I understand
Reactions are something
We can not plan
Empathy is not always
Immediately to hand

Sometimes words take time to form
And even longer
To land

PURPLE WARRIOR

The lads called me
Purple Warrior
Asked if my pubes matched my hair
Took piss out of my green Topshop shoes
I didn't care
I copied off my sister
So I knew it must be cool
That they dint know a thing about fashion
In this Kappa Slapper school
One Friday night
Down at Quack
The cock of year eleven
Gave me a piggy back
Span me round in circles
Chucked me on the grass
His lass wudda kicked-my-fuckin-head-in
If she'd've seen that
Blue Wicked sticky on my lips
I let him nick a kiss
He let me wear his tracky top
I let him feel my tits
He said
I like you cos you're different Vikki
And sometimes I'm the same
And then we went back to school on Monday
And we never spoke again

IN AND OUT

And we made our own fun dint we?
Yeah we did
Aged 13 and 10 Regal Kingsize and 1,2,3, 4...fucking yes! 6 quid!
And I can see us walking round Ferry. There we are, Jelly Baby
   tops, shiny skirts, home cut hair. Me orange face and you
   fishnet tights. Not allowed in cos your mam's bin on nights.
   And we can't go to mine cos my sister's a cow. So we stay
   together me and you.
We stay out.
Out. On cold concrete steps. Out. On the grandstand. Out. Of
   the way.
And I can see those little bottles of 20 20 in your army
   rucksack. Blue and pink. And I can hear them clink. And I
   can taste it on my lips. And I can feel us floating right out of
   Ferry. And we kick and kick and kick.
And one day, we were in.
In Creepy Chris' bedroom. In Slimy Steve's bath. In our music
   teacher's office. In it for the laughs. In secret or in trouble.
   In it too deep.
In the pit of my belly.
In the dorm when I'm asleep.
In darkness in the moment and in between my legs.
In the back of his car.
In his office. In his bed.
In the bath. In my diary.
In danger and in doubt.
In denial and invaded.

And then instantly, back out

JUST WALK AWAY

I take you to the train station toilets
in Leeds
and it takes longer than it should
for you to have a wee
a long complex routine
of tearing
and wiping and flushing and wiping and flushing
and today
tears leak as you go
at first a gentle moan
that grows raw
and animalistic
as though at any point
you might tip
grip my arm
kick
rip your hair from its roots and spit
And then you laugh
blast the taps
and interact
with the water

Mesmerised

as if it were the sea

You press the blowers
one for each hand
stand delighted

feel the tornado
sweep your soul
and love rage
from cave of your belly
like home

I flashback to Christmas day
normal families race cars in the park
You strip and leg it
and I restrain you on the grass
while you kick and punch
cry and laugh
folk look embarrassed
and I'm desperate for help
and nobody asks

A few years back
you rode feral and naked in my Jeep
I drove us to Mcdonald's after a night
of smearing and flooding and wailing
and 2 hours sleep
charged up with anger and ADHD
you opened the passenger door
and tried to jump free
enjoyed my fear
laughed hysterically at me

And every small step is huge
that time you joined a queue

and you waited in line
with the other kids
and I wondered if anyone would notice
your special needs
and nobody did

And I just wish that you'd fit in
and sometimes I'm glad you don't
you show me another way to live this life
you show me there is hope

So we carry on

Last week you smashed my tele
cos you rather things lay flat
at first I shouted then I cried
you must be used to that
and I love you

oh wow how I love you

That calm peaceful look
you get
when you tune right in
when your eyes connect with mine
and you let me in
the way you cheer with both hands and an open mouth
when you win

And sometimes we accidentally steal stuff from shops
cos there's not enough time to pay
you whizz through life
impatient
shoeless and sockless
twiddling and tapping
a toothbrush
clutching a
a bag of equally
inflated balloons
and today
you force feed me tangerines
lick your fingers and lips
and when we go for lunch
you sit nicely with your tablet
and watch
bouncy castles
and Paralympics

And I'm sorry for the times
when I've had enough
I see my mam up all night
Dogging on
Fucked
And I carry the weight
Of her disappointment
that I do not do
that feeling I am
not enough
to be of any use to you

I look around the train
at parents
tired with toddlers
at the end of their wick
and think how lucky they are
that theirs will grow out of it
That their exhaustion and frustration
is just a passing stage
that they can pick theirs up at any point
and
just
walk
away

CAN MAN

I wanted to write about the characters of
Knottingley
The Can Man
In his big blue house
On Hilltop
Up and down with his
Wheelbarrow
Full of scrap
One day
In Morrison's carpark
I asked if he could remember the time
He rescued our Christmas presents
From the skip
I said I wanted to capture his goodness
In my poem
And he told me this
He said
I am not a good man
No one is
He said
Once
As a kid
He wondered what would happen
If he took the budgie from its cage
And held down its wings
And shoved it head first through the
Cardboard inner tube of a toilet roll
While his mam n dad were out
And rolled it down the stairs

And he did
And it died
And he took it out
And put it back in

He said that humans are inherently wicked
And that we all live in sin

MILK BOTTLE TOPS

When I was a kid
We read Enid Blyton books
At the front
There was this bit about collecting milk bottle tops
For blind children
Does anyone else remember that?
I think that's what it said
I thought
They must stick those
Shiny silver buttons in their sockets
To make them
See again

SING LIKE ANGELS

Kids round here can't stand the silence
Kids round here buzz off the violence
Kids round ere live for excitement
Kids round ere are coiled
Kids round ere are poised

Kids round ere live for the noise
Kids round ere live for the noise

Kids round ere they spring like jacks
Kids round ere live for the laughs
Kids round ere with pushed up shoulders

March like soldiers
March like soldiers

Kids round ere live for explosions
Kids round ere live for the moment
Kids round ere get ard n sexy
Kids round here they take the piss
Kids round ere
"Wunt be seen dead in it"
Kids round ere they tut n spit
Tut n spit tut n spit
Kids round ere they take the piss
Kids round ere they
Tut n spit tut n spit

St Mary's church
Canterbury

I sit
Watch kids like this
Kids like this
Sing!
Kids still kids
Shoulders soft
Free of chips
Eyes wide n upturned lips
And I can't help but think
Poor things
Poor things'll
Get their fucking heads kicked in
Let it sink in
And realise
Kids like that
Aren't from round here
Kids like that don't live in fear
Kids like that are wrapped in arms
Kids round there are blessed with calm
Kids round there are safe
Kids round there are free
Kids round there are free
Kids round there are free from danger
Kids round there they sing like angels
Sing like angels
Sing like angels

Kids round there
They sing like angels

ALIVE

We climbed Gaddings Dam that night
In the dark
Your phone for a torch
Audre the greyhound
Pulling us up
Me
Flip flops
Long skirt hitched up
Bronte sisters
At dusk
Tripping up
Tripping up

But not turning back

And at the top we stood and watched
An empty black pool
Sparkling in the moonlight
Clear and cool
We stripped off and braved it
Me, the dog and you

And she was your magic sea horse
Your unicorn
Your stallion
And you were She Ra
My wild mermaid
My darling
Pooled in darkness

Showered in stars
Praying to the universe
On this night
To align us

How lucky I am
To have seen that
With these eyes

How lucky I am to have
Shared with you
that point in time

How lucky I am to
be here
Truly
Magnificently
Alive

BEST DRESS

I hang my blue silk dress on the back of my door
Wrap a scarf around the hanger
where your neck will be
Pin a sunflower to the breast

Today

You will wear my best dress

I've swapped it for something of yours
A red clip

I will wear it

And when I do
I will feel like you
Loud and bold

I will tell the story you wish
You could have told

I will wear you
Over and over
Until I'm old

I've filled two suitcases
With tears
and a bag
With all your clothes

ME AND YOU

Sometimes you were my mam
you'd fuss and hug
Soothe with
Those giant kind eyes
That had seen the same as me
And more
Those giant kind eyes
That were sorry and hollow
And sore
That downwards smile
That had learned to make do

in that town
where it was
Them and us

us and them
Me and you

LET IT BE

We bought pot noodles and protein bars
And packed up the van
Returned to the field in Chepstow
Where it all began
Six years ago
For my boys and me

Swam through poppy fields
And seas of green
And I hear you
Speaking words of wisdom
Directly to me
Reminding me who I am
And where I've been

And I can't believe it
My big lad
By my side
Golden curls gone now
But eyes twice as wide
Smile swooping like a seagull
Singing Let it be

And for five days in a field
The two of us are free

NAAANERRR

We had this pink Ghetto Blaster
And we could record our voice
on a tape
You liked us to sing songs that we could
Play back in the car
My Name is Tallula
I Should be so Lucky
When Will I Will I be Famous?
I am the One and Only
Sometimes I spoiled it on purpose
Near the end of the song
I was the youngest
I knew it was wrong
I had to take the power back where I could
One time
When grandma was babysitting
We pre-recorded ten minutes of us
Shouting
Nannnerrr
NAANNNERRRR
NAAAAAANNNNNNERRR
An overlapping cacophony of flat Five Town vowels
We played it at the top of the stairs
And hid behind your bedroom door
At first, "what? What?!"
Then we heard her crack and shout
"What?! Bloody hell!"
It was the funniest thing that ever happened in that house
Forgive us
It was the 80s
We were bored

SOMEONE WORSE OFF

Once at Leeds Festival
Someone tipped
A toilet over
With a girl inside
Maybe off her head on E
Door facing downwards
Trapped in the plastic stink of shit and heat
I thought

Thank fuck
Thank fuck
Thank fuck
It's not me

109

I eat salt and pepper chips on a wall by the ducks
I chuck a couple into the water and watch them fight
Everything will be alright
I've simplified life
I've stripped it right back to remove fuss
I walk into town
Travel back by bus
An older woman tuts
At the men swapping shift
"they're allers kalling them two"
She reminds me of my nanna
She can't see inside me
She doesn't know every frozen bone in me
Aches with grief
She tells me her routine with the 109
I am attentive
Grateful for the ease
She doesn't know what I've just seen
I'm glad for the time it takes
To board the bus
The days are long
I borrow books
Clean the oven
Bleach the cups

I wonder who else here
Is carrying their death in a doggy bag?
Wrapped up in a napkin for later

BOB

My mam took me to the hairdresser
And said "she wants a bob"
I didn't know what one was
Only that I wanted my hair
Like Mrs Spears'
But the hairdresser was odd
Even at age six
I knew something was wrong
For a start she was smoking
And we weren't in a salon
But in her house
And a baby kept crying
And she kept stopping
And I think she must have had a 1920s bob in mind
Because she cut it above my ears
Nothing at all like Mrs Spears'
About six inch shorter
And then I heard a buzzing
And she shaved it up the back

A pile of sad blonde curls cried on the carpet
And I was never the same again
After that

LET ME OUT

I made my words lean left like yours
You made every letter count
But you were screaming weren't you?

Let me out. Let me out. Let me out.

PLODDING ON

Plodders on
Plodding on
Waiting
For time to pass
While they tut and smoke and say
It's shit innit
Eh?
innit shit?
You can't win can you?
Eh?
Can't do rate for doin wrong
Aren't we alrate
And they say
Aye not so bad
Owd cock
Not so bad
Plodding on

SPUDS

I planted a spud
Shoved it deep
in a tub
Under a foot of mud
Then did what I do
left it
Watched it wither
And rot
But it still grew
Took up
Chunks of
Air
And the
Cragg vale
View
Unsightly and holy
Riddled with bugs
I gave up
But it knew
To keep on
Keep on
Keep on
Pushing through
And today
The day of truth
I stuck my hands
In deep
To be rid of you
And pulled

Up spuds
A full tub
Of you
Tiny pearls
And fat rocks
Of you
Washed you under the tap
And thanked
God for you
For not giving up
On me

THE ONE THAT PUSHED YOU IN

In the bathroom
The contractions start slow
Rise up my throat
Swell like a fungus
Grow
I surrender to the pain
Let it pull me back down to my knees
Again
I howl

In bed, I cuddle a cushion
Push it up against my belly
Like a body
To absorb sobs

And in the in-betweens
In the quiet calm
I notice
I am present
I notice
Nothing matters

I take every detail in
Every flicker every shadow on the ceiling

In silence
I am blown wide open
To Everything

A space woman
I transcend pain
I see every little thing:

That the force that pulled you out of the world
Is the same one that pushed you in

CATCH A POEM

I've come to catch a poem
Got a pack up of snap
And some gloves
And a net
I'm not sure what kind of poem
I'll be catching, yet

I know what I'm like
For catching
Those big heavy sad ones
Those ones weigh me down
Those ones
Wipe me out for days

I think the one I'll catch today will be light
One small enough to fit
In a tissue
Small enough
To be kept in a jar

It's is a tiny tiddler tadpole of a poem,
So far

It wants to say something

It wants to say something about
The sunshine today

It wants to say

How spring
And picnics
And good times
Are on the way

This poem wants to remind us
That we're not alone

I've caught it
I'll put the lid on
And take it home

DULL TONGUE

Lull me with your dull tongue
Wrap me up
Feel my belly combust
Flop like a loose balloon
Ease my vowels
Let them stretch West
Climb Black Hill
Come back to rest
Help me empty out my rucksack
And then pack back up

I shoved it all in wrong
Zipped stuff up in pockets
Years ago
Where they never
Belonged
Bunged in what I could
While the clothes were still damp

Lull me with your dull tongue, darling
Remind me who I am

GOOD ENOUGH

We sit in a circle
me and these lads
these tattooed
lassoed
scallywags
and I know them
quick as a click
Cos these are the lads of my youth
if I close my eyes
I'm back in school
back of the class
gobbing off
playing it cool
Or we're on the grandstand in the park
drinking mad dog 2020 before it even gets dark

These are the lost brothers of my tribe
those ones who fucked up
and fucked off
and ended up
banged up
inside

We sit and talk
they suss me out
and I tell them
everything
Stretch my heart and mind
wide open

I tell them
"You can do this
cos I'm imperfect too
and here's the best bit
in this class
the worse your stories
the better you'll do"
They pass around my book
and say
raight
nice
stuff
and make me feel
accepted
and within five minutes
we establish we are
equally respected
They talk about their birds in words never
heard about me
"I hope to fucking god she'll still be there
when I walk free"
and they talk in contradictions
this one lad, it's mad,
he dunt make the connection
would give you his last twenny P
this most generous, generous thief
And he sits and he's
fired up to fuck
and he tells me that

he can't feel emotions
I want to make him see
so I nod my head and agree
and try to implant these new thoughts
subliminally
I tell him
Mate
you can do whatever you want
if you believe
And then he tells me
why he likes to clean
that as a teen
he did it for his mam
and that he
made the tea
so she wunt get a hiding
when her fella got in
and then he runs
past me
this long loud fast list
of this and then this and then this and then this
expecting at the end that I must be truly convinced
that this lad here, this lad here can not feel

I tell him that I understand
that all those things
have been kept out to survive
but I tell him
if he starts to write

slowly, safely they can all come out
and if he'll let himself open
a little tiny bit
he might start to feel love
once he's cleared out some shit
And he sits and frowns
and he protests again
and I beam back
Wide
Eyed
Hope
and he picks up his pen

That lad opposite
is sensible and kind
he lost his baby
then lost his mind
'til hate burst from his fists
and all over a face
and two years later
he's got a qualification
in counselling
and he's grateful for this place
Some of them are
relieved to have had time
to let wounds heal and
form scars
and then the lad
to my right

He's the one
He's the one
I'll cry about when I'm in bed tonight
cos some of them get right in
your heart
and you're not entirely sure why
he's a man
with the wide eyed
dadless sadness of a young boy
and I tell him
Well done
Well Done
until it is embedded so deep
That he hears
"well done lad!" in his fucking sleep
and I tell him
please please please please
Replace
those harsh inner words
with new ones
speak to yourself like a child
like I've done
after years of
Bad lad
Bad lad
Slag
Shit mum
These can be our new ones:

We are good enough
We are good enough
We are good enough
We are good enough
We are good enough

I FORGIVE

I sat next to Loubi at your funeral
Me and your best girl

She took my hand and
Tucked it into her folded arms
I felt her belly convulse
Hard and fast like mine

Your coffin was a hand-woven basket
Rainbow striped
We lay sunflowers on top
And a magic eye
Your son, our dad and uncles
Carried you in
They played
"You've Got a Friend" by Carol King

At the end
Around your coffin
A semi circle of
Your kids

I kissed the wicker sticks
Around your head and whispered
"I forgive"

START LIFE AFRESH

Anew, again
Go on
Attach strings to your
Animated corporeal existence
and hand them over
Dance the fandango in
Your dad's Maroon Skoda
Pretend you never
No one cares
Enjoy
That period between
birth and death
Yes. Yes. Yes.
Forget about
The dead rabbits in the freezer
That game of slaps
Start life afresh
Burn out your old one
Like your dad's Maroon Rover
Chuck it
Like an Indian Takeaway
Polystyrene salad leftover
I would
Infact, fuck it, I have done
Go on
Start again
Begin again
At the end

STEPDAD

I think of me at Eden's age
And you at mine,
Listening to me
Play the same songs
Over n over n over again

Country House or Common People or The End

Weed smells from my bedroom
Locked door
Boyfriends

I wonder how you'd have parented me
If it had been up to you
I think you'd have been stricter
Than my mam allowed you to

I wish you had been able to say
No, Victoria,
Your boyfriend, who I do not know,
Absolutely cannot stay

I think I'm strict like you
And you would say
'you're doing a good job, cocker'
And you'd see me teach

I'm so sad
That you never really got to see me
Free

MAD

You were 15 and you had your own home
That's a mad age to be doing it alone
You bought big bottles of blackcurrant pop
From Aldi
For your bairne's
Boc boc juicies
Ironed his babygros

There was this kid who useda come round
Proud of the tab ends she'd found
For her mam's rollies

Tiny caterpillars
Hand unfurled
I'd never seen that world
before

I felt sad that you belonged to it now

But I liked your stories
About men who barbecued crows
Kept goldfish in the bath
About that lass and her mam who both smoked smack

We could never imagine a life like that

And you'd laugh
That piss tek laugh
Drag on your fag and tek it back
"Mad innit, girl.
Mad"

PERV

The gate at the bottom
Of my nanna's garden
Led to the allotments
At the back
You had to walk past Perv
And that water barrel
Where she'd drowned those cats
That was his name
It was strange because
We were told to stay away
But at the same time
My nanna made him cups of tea
He had his own cup
In her cupboard
On its own shelf
"That's Perv's cup, don't touch it"
She'd say

One day
Me and my friend
Were walking back
Perv stopped us and told us about
Some baby pigeons
Inside his shed
He said
We should go in and see
He shut the door behind us

Inside
A flutter and stink
A gurgling grey chaos

No baby birds

He said that they were
Unwanted
And that it was for
The best

To trick the pigeons
Into sitting
On artificial eggs

SECRETS

80s adverts were full of shit
You could never do the stuff
That they said you could with it
We both had Keepers
And we still thought they were good
But you couldn't hide
Your secrets
Like they made you think you could

CALLOTS

One summer
Our nanna made us callots
I hadn't heard that word
A lot
The kids at school dint say it
My mam said it meant
Baggy shorts

She'd whizzed them up quick
On the sewing machine
Quick quick quick
Like everything she did

One Saturday
In the living room
They made me try them on
They all started laughing
I wondered what was wrong

The material off Ponte market
Bought in a rush:

Two cows shagging
And some writing that said

"muchas gracias"

Thankyou very much

HERE THEY COME

Remember when it snowed in Holmfirth?
The vast whiteness of everything
The feeling of purity it would bring
The relief that now it's not just us
Stuck in

Remember their bright pink noses the shovels the cuddles the
    fires the curly blonde hair
I want to forget about
the bangs and smoke
the armlock on the Salvation Army chair

I want to feel the best bits
I know they're in there
I want to remember so I can say
Remember that day or this day or this day

I've drawn a thick black border around the trauma
Turned it black and white and made it still
Reduced it to a postage stamp
Turned the volume down until

I can see his angry face but tiny as a pin
And I'm laughing now at how miniscule
He is
And I'm not scared of him
His violence is silent as a

I could flick him off a table
Like a pea
I could sneeze and blow him away
Far far away from them
And us
And me

I've made space for good memories to float up
I wait with an open photo book
Tongue clicks them in
Daft dogs run
I wait with arms wide open

Good boy good boy good boy
Here they come

FULL UP

Bellies full of Yorkshire puddings
and meat
Bellies round and soft
lips sweet

I remember when it was just me

And watch the three of you now
Full up
Sleep

RED SHOES

A bright yellow light
Lit up the sign
Rhodes and Son
Our stage
In the Chapel of Rest
Carpark on Weeland Road
Next door to where we lived
Where we'd perform our best moves
On rollerboots
For passing cars
Re-enact Hans Christian Handerson's
Tale of the Red Shoes
Those ones you laced up too tight
Could never remove
Those ones that
Made you dance and dance
'Til you had nothing left

Those ones that danced you and danced you and danced you
To death

WHEN YOU SEE MEN

When you see men
Imagine them
With their head
between your legs

Remember who birthed them

When you see men

EARS

Little curls of things
Pink shells on your head
You hear the sea
When you lay in bed
Yes you
Fun sprung
Quick triggered
A burst of
Too loud too soon too much
Daftness

Exasperated,
I implode

In your absence
I near explode
With love

GOOD MAM

Son,
Today you are twelve
Two giant silver balloons
A one and a two
Suspended
Like moons
A daft animal song plays by accident
Instead of Happy Birthday
And I laugh
For once
I'm not crushed by imperfection
Infact
I prefer it

Your brother says
"cos it's your birthday you can punch me on t'arm"
And you do
And the birthday buzz is snuffed like a candle
He cries and you're too hard on yourself
You've learned that from me
But this time
I don't react
Today I am older too
Instead I respond
From a place of love
Hold space for peace and calm
And like all pain it passes
With acceptance, forgiveness and strong arms

We go for out for breakfast
Tell tales over toast
A waitress tells me about her son
We talk about
All
Our
Sons
The ones we
Mother
On behalf of others
She says
"I can tell you're a good mam"
And for the first time
I let it land
I am
I am
I am

PARSNIP DAY

This morning
I made pancakes for breakfast
They were mostly shit
But we had a laugh
Ember ate blue food colouring
and twerked and that

You asked me to
Take you
To a proper pancake shack
I told you to wrap up
And of course
You didn't listen
Found yourself
On yonder moor
Exposed and freezing

On the way back
Ember bought you
A bag of parsnips
From the shop
We don't know why
he does stuff like that
He said they were reduced

You bit into one
And spat it out the window
down the side of the car
And there are many times
That would have been
One parsnip
Too far

But today I laughed
and you love me a bit more
and I've left a bit of parsnip
as a reminder
on the door

TEACHERS

Those teachers at school
You could blag into
Letting you skive
By asking questions
About stuff you knew
They couldn't resist but answer
You were killing time
They were at their
Most alive
Miss Stringer
The Beatles
Miss Booth
Egypt
Miss Millington
Bjork

Pens down
Stretch
Watch
Them

Talk

ELEPHANTS

I wish I could drive through space
Back to 2003
For just one day
And you'd be in the kitchen
In your old place
Kettle on constant boil
Hoovering
Earning a burn
For us both
Hole on loud
Your son
Neatly pressed
House clean
House proud
Loud and gobby
Everything polished
And we'd sit
Holding elephants in
Tight
Tigers flashing teeth and claws
Sometimes
And you'd dance
Penguin arms
Bounce around
Your magpie's nest
Take the piss
do impressions
make me laugh
in spite of myself

And you'd say
"fuck him, Toy, he's a dick"
And you were always right

I wish I could let the elephants out
and make everything alright

FUNERALS FOR BIRDS

When I was 7 and you were 9
You got into this new thing
You had us looking round
The fields at the back
Of our house
For dead birds

It started at Grandma's one weekend
We found a crow in the
Allotment
And carried it back
What was it about that day? That crow?
That made you want to do that?

You were in charge
I did as you said
Fetched supplies
To the greenhouse
Where the service was being held

And you wrapped it up
Like a mummy
In toilet roll
Made a cross out of lolly sticks
and dug a hole

You were serious and sombre
And I was a silly next to you
impressed that

You always knew
Exactly what to do

We said The Lord's prayer
And then a few words of our own
You said
"Please dear God look after this crow"

I laughed and pissed you off
More than I could understand

And then we ate a ten pence mix up
Without washing our hands

SISTERLESS

Last night you came to me in my sleep
We were together again
Like 2003
I'd forgotten that version of us
Ever existed
We were
In the charity shop
Smoking
Doing
Buy one get one free
You know
And I know
That means summat else
To you an me
We sang to Moldy Peaches
Earner burners, cups of tea
I said
I'm sorry for the shit things
I did to you
And you were sorry too
And we held
eachother
Harder
Than our mam
Could ever do
And then we slept
In a bed
Cuddled up like
bairnes on Fairburn Ings again

And in the morning
you had to go
But you wouldn't let me see
Said that world was
Too much too dark too soon
For me
And I begged you to stay
But you had
No choice
No more

And I woke up in the real world
More sisterless
Than before

WISH YOU WERE HERE

I hear waves of your wild choking laugh
Like a toothbrush turning on and off
Underneath the bongos
And Hare Krishnas
Pissing yourself at the Laughing Yoga
Taking the fucking piss

And Scunny Pete is your mate
You see Roachy in his face
Like me
You belong
To woodland and campfires
To cups of tea
Fairy lights
The Free Shop

I ache to have you here with me

Wrapped in a blanket in the back of my van
I say it out loud
"I wish you were here, An"
And you say

"I am"

Toria was born in Knottingley in 1982. She currently lives in Mytholmroyd with her two sons.

Photo: Emma Aylett